Jacob Edson

Our Articles of Faith

A brief statement of self-evident truths, exhibiting the foundation of the broad church

Jacob Edson

Our Articles of Faith
A brief statement of self-evident truths, exhibiting the foundation of the broad church

ISBN/EAN: 9783337090357

Printed in Europe, USA, Canada, Australia, Japan

Cover: Foto ©Lupo / pixelio.de

More available books at **www.hansebooks.com**

OUR ARTICLES OF FAITH.

A BRIEF STATEMENT OF

SELF-EVIDENT TRUTHS,

EXHIBITING THE

FOUNDATION OF THE BROAD CHURCH, ITS CHRIST, "WHICH LIGHTETH EVERY MAN THAT COMETH INTO THE WORLD."

A COMPENDIUM OF RELIGION; "THE SUBSTANCE OF THINGS HOPED FOR, THE EVIDENCE OF THINGS SEEN."

BY

JACOB EDSON.

BOSTON:
IRA BRADLEY & CO.
No. 20 WASHINGTON STREET.
1873.

ARTICLES OF FAITH.

DEDICATION.

THE age demands a statement of religion that shall be brief, simple, comprehensive and explicit; that shall include, comprehend, and demonstrate all the truths that have sought expression in the systems of the past in such a manner as to unfold, harmonize, and bless the race. Believing that such a system of religion exists in the divine mind, and is about to be made known, we feel it to be our privilege, as well as duty, to do what little we can to prepare the way for its unfoldment. With this object — this aim in view — these articles have been written; to this end they are now dedicated.

CONTENTS.

	PAGE.
PREAMBLE	9

ARTICLE I.
Flowers — Their Culture and its Effect. 10

ARTICLE II.
Love — What It Is — Its Universal Aim and Its True Spontaneity. 11

ARTICLE III.
Religion as distinguished from Theology and Speculations — The Progress of the Soul — Its Final Unfoldment into the Likeness of God 14

ARTICLE IV.
The Tree of Life — The Kingdom of Heaven — Its Dividing Line — the Wigwam, and How to Find It . 20

ARTICLE V.
Theology the Soul of Science — Its Functions — The *Isms* of Religion the Only Preventive — The Bible, and Other Religious Books — Moses in Egypt, and the Sepulchre of the Soul 26

ARTICLE VI.
The Subjective World — The Judgment-seat of Christ — The Receptivities of the Soul — The Border States — The Kingdom of Heaven, and the How we are to Enter It 34

ARTICLE VII.

The Path of Peace — How We are Brought into It — Regeneration Illustrated — The Reason why so Few are being Converted to Christianity — the Love of Genuine Goodness, and what the Lovers Should Do ... 38

ARTICLE VIII.

Love Opposed to Bondage — The Truly Good Man — A "Sweet Sinner" and a "Sour Saint," and the Remedy for their Troubles ... 44

ARTICLE IX.

Teachings of Jesus — Vicarious Atonement — The Murderer on the Gallows — Love of Jesus — The Infernal Abode, and the Glory of God in the Regeneration of Man ... 48

ARTICLE X.

The Christian Religion — Joseph's Coat — Christianity from an Intellectual Standpoint — Religious Persecution — Ingersoll in Search of the Gods, and the Work he is doing ... 53

ARTICLE XI.

Christianity Not a Failure — The Law of Life — The First and Second Coming of the Christ — Prayer Illustrated — The Condition of our Country — What is Recommended — What should Be Done, and How to Do It — Our Final Home ... 66

ARTICLE XII.

Our Belief Defined — Truth — Its Effect — Nature — God's Mode of Operation — The Harmony of the Spheres — The Journey of Life Illustrated — Reputation and Character — Darwinism — Freedom and its Effects ... 104

PREAMBLE.

SOLITUDE and silence, that can be felt as described by Kane in the vicinity of the pole, is the state, the condition to perceive and appreciate truth.

To be alone, is to be with God. Perfect rest is perfect action; it is the Eden of life — the finality from which we come to which we hasten.

From a subjective standpoint, the constitution of man is a divine enactment. The spiritual by-laws that bind and hold him to his Creator include, permeate, and control all the states and conditions of life, so that the so-called incidents and accidents that continually beset and befall us are made to unfold and perfect the Christ, in the heart and consciences, the will and the understanding, which constitutes the wisdom of the race.

ARTICLE I.

FLOWERS — THEIR CULTURE AND ITS EFFECT.

WE believe in the divinity of Flowers,—that their study and culture tend to unfold the beauties of nature and the capacities of the soul.

Not only flowers, but buds, as well as blossoms, bespeak the coming Spring, and tell of harvest. Winter, as well as Autumn, has its charms. Not only the seasons, but the months in the seasons, allegorically illustrate the truth of Holy Writ.

"Stars and flowers are sisters"; they reveal the beauty of God in nature, and reflect His glory above.

ARTICLE II.

LOVE — WHAT IT IS — ITS UNIVERSAL AIM AND ITS TRUE SPONTANEITY.

WE find in every man's life a chord which, touched by a kindred sympathetic vibration, thrills and echoes through the inmost fibres of our own souls. Clinging to this, each and every human being urges his way on in life; find where it is attached, and you have a clew, following which, you can trace each step the man has trod, and divers mazes, unnatural wanderings, and explicable contradictions become the clear and necessary results of easily-defined law. It is the law of Love — mysterious influence — evidencing its divine origin, yea, more, its inherent divinity, in its universal adaptation to all conditions of men.

Love is to the soul what magnetism is to the compass — the motive-power which directs all its actions; what blood is to the animal, or sap to vegetable life — the channel of communication; yes, the very element itself of growth and vitality; ay, all, and above all, and more than all, it is to the human soul what God is to the universe — the life thereof. "God is Love," — the allegorical tree of life implanted in the hearts and consciences of men.

"Love, sanctified by religion, can never die;" "it is too delicate a plant to thrive in the chilly atmosphere of neglect; let it be warmed by the breath of a pure affection, and it will grow and thrive, giving forth beauty, fragrance, and fruit." "Not always can flowers, pearls, poetry, protestation, nor even home, content the unfolding soul that dwells in clay; it arouses itself, at last, from these endearments, as toys, and puts on the harness, and aspires to vast and universal aims. "The great end and aim of life is to become united to God, that His service may be our joy, His presence our perpetual home." "The essential elements of a true home are not confined to the few, but opened to the many; home is too rich a boon to be monopolized by any class, or limited to any external condition of men." "Trust not the spontaneity of love; the fountains play freely only when the reservoir is full, and the reservoir soon fails when the little rills, rivulets, springs, and streams, gushing out of the mountain-side, are cut off. It is the thousand little mossy droppings, pearly rills, and hidden springs of living affection, gushing out of the sunny slopes, shady retreats, and rocky glens of every-day life, that give to the fountain of love its true spontaneity."

There is a stream, a peaceful stream,
   From Heaven within it flows;
It warms and urges on in life
   The soul through whom it glows.

'Tis broad and deep, 'tis calm and clear,
   The stream from Heaven runs still;
'Tis ever onward in its course,
   Its mission to fulfil.

ARTICLE III.

RELIGION AS DISTINGUISHED FROM THEOLOGY AND SPECULATIONS — THE PROGRESS OF THE SOUL — ITS FINAL UNFOLDMENT INTO THE LIKENESS OF GOD.

RELIGION is the spiritual manifestation of the Divine principle of Love implanted in the human soul; it involves the knowledge of "good and evil," their unfoldment, the passional nature, its "flaming swords," and the final partakement of "the Tree of Life." As distinct from Theology, it is godliness, or real piety in practice; as distinct from virtue or morality, it consists in the performance of the duties we owe directly to God — from a principle of obedience to His will, the term implies bondage — being bound anew not to any particular theory or creed, but to truth, by faith reposed in certain ideas; its object is to unfold motives for action, derived from an acknowledgment of Divine power, rather than to indicate any particular line of conduct itself. It is a bond of union which unfolds the principle of Love, and lifts the soul to God.

This definition excludes from the domain of religion proper all mere conceptions of the nature, attributes, and purposes of God; all mere perceptions of the capabilities, opportunities, and necessities of man, these proofs of intellectual capacity and advancement it gives over to their proper place, belonging, as they do, to speculation, which must ever be the handmaid of a living religion, and in this capacity must be useful; but which, as a substitute for religion, can be only baneful in its results.

Correct speculation — I mean unprejudiced inquiry in a receptive spirit — tends to increase the inquirer's knowledge of God, to unfold and blend his affections in closer bonds of love to Him, thus bringing God nearer the man while it raises him nearer his Creator.

The unprogressed soul may be considered an eternal distance of unregenerated love and affection; from its divine cause, his ineffable presence, this distance constitutes the journey of life. In going godward, we distinguish between the development of the faculty of the soul, and the progression of the soul that possesses the faculty; the one is the capacity to do, the other is the thing done. The reward is not for, but in the doing, " to be or not to be " blest is not so much a question of time, place, or capacity, as it is a question of states and conditions. Prayer, in its best sense, is spiritual demand : its answer, divine supply.

Experimental religion involves the conception and development of inspired conditions — the practical entering into, and coöperation with, the power that is both demand and supply; capacity to receive is the limit of power to bestow. "His arm is not shortened, that He cannot save." But our condition may be such, that salvation for the time being is impossible. Repentance is not so much an act, as it is a state, a condition, that precedes and produces action; it is not inconsistent with the infinite perfection of the Omniscient to make this blessing dependent upon the action of the recipient.

Let the sceptic question the necessities of his own soul to deny the efficacy of prayer *in toto*. To hold that the unchangeable God cannot be moved in accordance with His will, leads at once and directly to the doctrine of Fatalism, which, believed in, renders the soul apathetic, and incapable of effort or advancement. To allow a reflex benefit to the soul from communing with God but advances a step higher, though it opens a way and motive for improvement, and gives abundant reason why men ought always to "pray, and not to faint," but to hold God a sympathizing Father, ever ready to hear the cry of His children — a wise and beneficent Creator, who has made the bestowment of His favors dependent upon our efforts — leads to a filial trust, to a warm, gushing love, and a life of devotion to His service.

This idea, gloriously adapted to the wants of the human soul, is the only one by which may be produced the effect each man knows he needs; nor is such idea unreasonable, nor is such a course a mark of fickleness of mind on the part of God. His laws are ever the same. His providences are ever-varying; — the latter always adapted to the circumstances and conditions of the persons influenced. As well accuse Him of fickleness of mind, because, from the same soil, expanded by the same sun, watered by the same showers, two plants grow side by side as dissimilar as the rose and the violet. As well accuse Him of inconsistency, because the acorn, planted in the deep soil, expands into the splendid oak; while another, dropped in the crevice of some granite rock, becomes a mere scrubby shrub.

True religion may be defined to be a life of receptive trust in the providence of God. The soul may be considered a divine plant receiving its substance from God; and if we allow cares, trials, frivolity, and speculations to engross our whole time, and as rocks to prevent the tendrils of our hearts from taking hold on Him, or as choking weeds to hinder the leaves of desire from expanding in the sunlight of His countenance, we cannot expect a vigorous growth. If we cut off the tender fibrils which crowd the roots, we cannot look for beauteous blossoms. As well hide the material plant from the natural sun, and expect to gather the luscious fruit, as to deprive the soul of spiritual communion and religious associations, and hope a glorious development.

The religions that have preceded us have served the purposes of divine economy, as means to ends, in the order they obtained.

As the monkey and the ape, as well as the lion and the lamb, preceded man in the order of creation, so the more cruel and barbarous religions preceded and made possible the more human and divine religions of to-day, which in their turn must give way to the ever-unfolding Word.

Cut man loose from the object of his affection, or the religion that bound him, without giving him a new point to which to attach himself, and he straightway falls into a pit of despair; induce him day by day to fix his affections on more and still more worthy objects, and step by step he approaches nearer and nearer, and reflects more and more clearly, the image of the Perfect God.

There's a fount beyond the river;
'Tis the source of all our joy:
From it flows, in love forever,
Perfect good without alloy.

ARTICLE IV.

THE TREE OF LIFE — THE KINGDOM OF HEAVEN — ITS DIVIDING LINE — THE WIGWAM, AND HOW TO FIND IT.

THE tree of life — the kingdom of heaven — is within you; the grain of mustard-seed — the pearl of great price — is there; the Bible is a pictorial exhibition of its unfoldment; if we read it as poetry, it is beautifully expressive of truth adapted to almost every conceivable condition in life; but if we read it as prose, we materially injure or entirely destroy its teachings. The background of the picture is dark animal passions, contention, and strife, enkindled by self-love, breaking forth and bursting out like volcanoes. The idea of a wrathful and vindictive God everywhere abounds. The Decalogue is inscribed upon the tablets of the human soul amid the thunder of Mount Sinai; the meekest of men is mad with anger in his effort to transmit the record; the tables of stone, as well as the golden calf, are broken to pieces. The Jewish fathers tremble with fear; they accept and serve, as best they can, their highest ideal of the one only and true God. It is a slavish service, unworthy of a different age. Through the sacrificial blood of bulls and goats they appeased, so far as their conscience is concerned, the wrath of an offended God. He hears their cry, inspires their thought. Poetic teaching and prophetic prose unfold the nation; a new era dawns upon the race; the star of Bethlehem reflects its light — the Christ — the quickened spirit obtains, as an entity in man; the sentiment of forgiveness, because of Ignorance, becomes a reality in human experience. The fact that *love*, and not blood, is the substance that saves, begins to be understood; it is the dividing line between daylight and darkness, night and day, good and evil. On the one hand is war, contention, and strife: the ring-streaked and speckled fighting religionists, literal believers in absolute evil, total depravity, and eternal torment; on the other hand is love, joy, and peace, the priesthood of Melchisedec, believers in the goodness of God and the sonship of the race; it is the gospel of *peace* — a love-letter to all mankind; as much so to the merest blotch of humanity that now mars the otherwise fair face of God in nature (if he could only see it), as to the genial, loving soul that sings in harmony with angels the psalms of life.

We do not believe that any human soul can be irrecoverably lost; it may be we all have been at fault, and bewildered. We have found ourselves on the wrong road, going the wrong way, a great ways off from our father's house, years ago, allegorically speaking; we used to carry a guide-board with us, but found out, after a long and painful experience, that a guide-board was of little use except for the state and condition for which it was painted.

"It is the wigwam, and not the Indian, that is lost."

The germ of divine life is within you, like Lazarus in the tomb, or the oak in the acorn, waiting conditions.

We are told that by properly conditioning a bar of common iron, and striking it a few sharp, quick blows, we can awaken within it a latent power, a magnetic force, that will indicate its relation to the poles, and serve the purpose of a compass; not that it will be as correct or efficient as can be made from properly-prepared and polished steel, but sufficiently so to enable the lost mariner or woodsman to find his way home. As with the bar of iron, so with the human soul. There are none so low down in the scale of being but what, if spoken to under proper conditions, if touched in the right spot, will respond to the call and come forth; or, like the acorn properly conditioned, will spring into life, and, growing under the sunshine of an infinite cause, will ripen into perfect fruit.

It is said that by placing bars of common iron, properly conditioned, each to the other, and all to the poles, that they in time will become receptive to, and surcharged with the electric force of the planet, so as to exhibit the power that controls the universe. As with bars of iron, so with human souls, properly conditioned, each to the other, and all to God, we may in time become not only receptive to, and surcharged with, but the channel itself of communion and fellowship unfolding and fructifying the allegorical vine and vintage of the Lord.

Qualities of love and affection differ and distinguish each of us from all others; it constitutes our individuality, which can never be lost. As the lily, the violet, and the rose differ in color, form, and fragrance, so we, plants of the immortal garden, must ever possess, and continue to unfold and perfect, the peculiarities implanted within. If we keep company with the violet and the rose in our communion with God, we partake of their nature; which, added to our own, constitutes a trinity of life — of unfolding progression in capacity to perceive, appreciate, and enjoy what could not have been without such differences and partakement.

Truth is the natural food of the soul; it sustains and unfolds our metaphysical bodies. Thought is to the thinker what walking is to the walker — it moves him from where he stood. Though we may not, by taking thought, add to our stature, we may, by taking thought, discover how small we are, and be induced to let go the creeds and dogmas that belittle and stultify us. In short, it is by thought, experience, observation and practice that we are enabled to perceive, appreciate, and become receptive to teachings, states and conditions very much superior to us. In this consists the science of godliness, — it is in accordance with nature, — it is God's mode of operation, allegorically speaking. The very worms beneath our feet are crawling up towards higher forms of existence, going godward, being crushed into more and still more perfect expression of life.

THERE is a hope, a cheering hope,
   The anchor of the soul:
It holds our hearts in love to God
   As magnets to the pole.

*   *   *   *   *

There is a love, a light, a life,
   None but the true can know:
'Tis Charity, that perfect good,
   Which God alone can show.

ARTICLE V.

THEOLOGY THE SOUL OF SCIENCE — ITS FUNCTIONS — THE ISMS OF RELIGION THE ONLY PREVENTIVE — THE BIBLE, AND OTHER RELIGIOUS BOOKS — MOSES IN EGYPT, AND THE SEPULCHRE OF THE SOUL.

THEOLOGY is the soul of science; it is unfolded upon, as well as implanted within, the rock of ages. It includes, amplifies, and compliments all the arts and sciences. Its function is to transplant, or rather unfold and transform, the flowers — the blossoms of earth — into the fruitage of heaven; to transmute the baser metals of our nature into gold — the godliness of eternal good. In other words, to analyze, reveal, and demonstrate the presence and transforming power of God in the hearts and consciences of men; it is the science of godliness in theory and practice.

Doctors of divinity have been supposed to know all the spiritual maladies and malformations the human soul is liable to; but we find, by observation and experience, that they, in common with others, treat symptoms rather than the disease itself — that they do not always understand the cause and cure. In short, that they, in common with ourselves, are troubled with the same complaint — ignorance — in some of its different forms of manifestation; not alone the ignorance of the head, the intellect, the understanding, which our theological schools and colleges are calculated to eradicate, but also the ignorance of the heart, its affections, the will, its "upper standing," which enables one to walk with God.

Different *pathists* have obtained and practised upon our credulity, but none, not even the homœopathists, have successfully treated all the complaints that have been and can be made. The eclectic and optimistic have been the most successful; they seem to be more radical, to enter more thoroughly into the merits of the case; they usually prescribe Time and Common Sense, to which we would add the quickening of the spirit and the inspiration of the Almighty. Most of the regular faculty prescribe Religion, which we accept; possibly we should not recommend their peculiar stripe, or any especial ring-streak or speckle. Most of the regular professors speak of religion as though it was something to be got or had, like a contagious disease, and not as something inherent in man, as taught by the Christ.

We grant that the *isms* of religion are contagious; that we are all liable to them, in certain stages of development, but they are not dangerous in these times. Occasionally one becomes creed-ridden — loses his capacity to think, and settles down into sectarian bigotry. None die — they simply cease to live for the time being, their worship becoming a mere mill-work, like the Connecticut nutmeg; externally, looking very much like the real, but internally, heartless, — very unlike the kind that grow.

We know of but one preventive, — a thorough infusion of truth in every conceivable line of theological thought and metaphysical speculation; a thorough partakement of the tree of life, the different parts of the metaphysical body of God; a deep and continued draught at the fountain of life; an entire and complete immersion in the boundless ocean of eternal love; a baptism of which Baptists need not be ashamed.

The *isms* and creeds of religion are "but skins of truth stuffed and set up," — they serve the purpose of steps and gates at the entrance of spiritual life ; but it is not until we have passed the phase of denominational distinction, that we discover how large a place it is. Getting religion is a process of unfoldment, and not an event to occur and be recorded like the birth, marriage, or death of an individual ; there are discrete conditions of goods and truths, successive conceptions of, and births into, views — ways and means which make up and constitute the journey of life.

We should as soon think of saying we had got mathematics, music, poetry, or the art of money-making, as to say we had got religion, or were a professor. What propriety would there be in calling the young student, who had but just learned that there was such studies as the arts and sciences, a professor of them, much less in calling an individual a professor of religion — the soul of all science — when he had but just discovered the existence of his religious nature, its origin, relation, and destiny? It is more than an impropriety to presume upon our profession of religion in a dogmatic and dictatorial manner, that we, because of certain experiences and vicarious interconjunctions, are saints, in contradistinction to this or that so-called sinner who is earnestly investigating the law of life, and, in his straightforward up-and-down honesty, is truthful enough to say that he can't see it (religion) in the light we do; it is an insult to common sense, of which dogmatic theology has reason to be ashamed.

We would not ignore the value of experience, or the law of sympathy which binds each to the other, and all to God. It is possible so to sympathize with the bound, as to get the advantage of their bondage; without its slavish chain, there is an interconjunction of soul through which one lifts himself by lifting others; no one can be perfectly at home in heaven until his entire generation is lifted out of hell. Such is the solidarity of the race, that if one man is lifted up in the best sense of that term, he must lift all men up with him.

Religious experience, observation, and practice may not make an individual interiorly any better; it unfolds his better self — the divine principle implanted within — and puts him into a position to aid others.

Theological teachings, as depicted in the sacred

books of the world, are threefold in their nature and modes of interpretation: like the chestnut, they have an external husk, an interior shell, and the meat, or life-giving substance, within. The outer protects the inner, and enables the inmost to unfold and demonstrate itself; the thing demonstrated we call revealed religion — the soul of science. The particular fold we are enabled to perceive and appreciate, depends upon the progress we have made, the standpoint we occupy, in the journey of life. This idea may be illustrated by the picture of Moses in the rushes; it is a trinity of views in one picture, not unlike the allegorical statement of Father, Son, and Holy Ghost. The scoffing sceptic, not yet having (so far as his conscience is concerned) commenced the journey of his religious life, sees nothing in the picture but a dreary marsh, a mere waste of coarse vegetation. From this standpoint the exact sciences grind the statements of the Bible and other religious books to powder, and scatter their teachings as chaff before the wind. He perceives only the husks of truth; it is the negative state of existence, or, if positive, is on the dark side of nature. Enlighten his understanding, open his spiritual perception, and he will discover a lion upon the marsh, — it is the lion of the tribe of Judea. If he be true to his perceptions in this plane of thought, he will be fixed as a flint, and will strike fire upon every piece of theological steel that comes in his path. It is the blood of bulls and goats that atones for sin, and saves the sinner, in that department of nature; it is the shell of truth — it is the father in the allegorical trinity — he has discovered, and is contending for. Enlighten him still further, and he will perceive the lamb. It is so conditioned that the lion is not in view; it is mysterious to behold. The picture has not been changed, but the man is transformed, or rather is in the process of transformation. He knows the lion is there lying in the way; blood is still the element of communion, — not the blood of bulls and goats, but the blood of the Son of God — the second figure in the godhead. Lead him on still further in the journey of life, and from another, a more interior and distinct standpoint, he will discover the allegorical child, — the third person in the godhead, the veritable Moses in Egypt; — the Christ of God — the Holy Ghost — the gate of heaven — yea, heaven itself; in short, that quality of love and affection, without which repentance is of little avail.

The different phases of unfoldment were but the rolling away of the stone from the sepulchre of his own soul, in which the truth was buried, so that the Christ, the quickened spirit, could come forth and demonstrate its existence as the soul of science in the hearts and consciences of the race.

"Hath not thy heart within thee burned
 At evening's calm and holy hour,
As if its inmost depths discerned
 The presence of a loftier power?

. Hast thou not heard 'mid forest glades,
 While ancient rivers murmured by,
A voice from forth the eternal shades,
 That spake a present Deity?

And as, upon the sacred page,
 Thine eye in rapt attention turned
O'er records of a holier age,
 Hath not thy heart within thee burned?

It was the voice of God that spake
 In silence to thy silent heart;
And bade each worthier thought awake,
 And every dream of earth depart."

ARTICLE VI.

THE SUBJECTIVE WORLD — THE JUDGMENT-SEAT OF CHRIST — THE RECEPTIVITIES OF THE SOUL — THE BORDER STATES — THE KINGDOM OF HEAVEN, AND THE HOW WE ARE TO ENTER IT.

There is a subjective as well as an objective world; man is a microcosm of all that preceded him — an epitome of all that is to come after. It is not necessary to go outside of ourselves to find a wrathful God, a burning hell, where "the worm dieth not, and the fire is not quenched." In our unprogressed sphere the ignorance of the heart, the affections, will create the place, and furnish the fuel to burn. Progression, as defined, walking with God, as described, will move us out of its existence. In the sphere above us there is no occasion or cause to produce it; on the sunny side of nature all things are fair and bright. Untried innocence does not develop the highest form of virtue, or bring the repentant sinner to the judgment-seat of Christ. It is a beautiful theme for contemplation, this judgment-seat of Christ; that state of intuitive perception, that quality of love and affection, that sees into and sympathizes with the bound as bound with them, that knows not only the how and the wherefore, but the extent to which we were damned, so far as damnation is possible, in the mothers that bore us — the conditions that preceded us — before we were born. How different the sentiment of the Christ from that of Moses. The last words of David, the representative figure in the law of fear and force, were, "Solomon, my son, thou art a wise man"; referring to Joab, who had done him a personal injury, he said, "Bring down his gray hairs in sorrow to the grave"; the last words of Jesus, the representative figure in the law of love, speaking to the Christ, that He felt had forsaken Him, were, "Lord, forgive them, for they know not what they do."

Theology, as the soul of science, is a gladsome, joyous study; it has to do with our affectional nature — the receptivities of the soul; it unfolds the subjective world, and demonstrates the personal existence and power of God in the transformation of the race.

There are border states through which the soul must pass in the journey of life; it is a disputed territory, where guerilla warfares are carried on. It is the manifestation of the leaven in the measures of meal. It is so to be, resistance does not avail us anything; it rather exhausts than develops the capacities of the soul. In that state we may join all the peace societies in existence, and discuss most learnedly the question of non-resistance; we may go further, and, so far as our external selves are concerned, be the meekest of men; but the spirit of anger is within, and controls us. The tables must be broken — the barriers of eternal truth must obtain — the foundations of a higher life must be laid down deep below the muds of animalism — the abutments of the bridge that spans the gulf between the animal and the divine man, and connects the material with the spiritual universe, must be reared — we must subjugate within ourselves the entire animal kingdom; all the "ring-streaked and speckled," "the lion and the lamb," must lie down together, so that the little child — the third person in the trinity — can lead them, in us, up into the kingdom of heaven, where all is love, joy, and peace.

"There is a land mine eye hath seen,
   In visions of enraptured thought,
So bright that all which spreads between
   Is with its radiant glory fraught; —

A land upon whose blissful shore
   There rests no shadow, falls no stain;
There those who meet shall part no more,
   And those long parted meet again.

There sweeps no desolating wind
   Across that calm, serene abode;
The wanderer there a home may find
   Within the Paradise of God."

ARTICLE VII.

THE PATH OF PEACE — HOW WE ARE BROUGHT INTO IT — REGENERATION ILLUSTRATED — THE REASON WHY SO FEW ARE BEING CONVERTED TO CHRISTIANITY — THE LOVE OF GENUINE GOODNESS, AND WHAT THE LOVERS SHOULD DO.

"THERE is a path which no fowl knoweth, which the vulture's eye hath not seen." "It cannot be gotten for gold, neither shall silver be weighed for the prize thereof"; "the lion's whelps have not trodden it"; "God understandeth the way thereof," "and the thing that is hid bringeth he forth to light."

Activity is a necessity. Discovery is the result. The young man starts out in life in the service of Mammon, seeking gold. Chains of circumstances, over which he has little or no control, switch him off the track; he finds himself a very different creature from what he was. The leopard's spots, the Ethiopian's skin, have been changed, through the workings of the law of regeneration, within him. He is now running an up-grade in the service of God, seeking a higher life. "We are moved wiser than we know."

We are told by agricultural chemists that great droughts are necessary at times; that they enable an electric substance, an essential element, to come up from the subsoil below, to vivify, unfold, and perfect the vegetable kingdom. As with the soil of earth, so with the soul of man: the divine principle of love seeks for a more and still more perfect form of expression.

We are told that by cutting off the seed part of the coarser grains, and not allowing them to mature, we may produce a different order — a higher grade. It has been demonstrated always with the same results (oats under this treatment will produce rye), showing the existence of the law of regeneration. We are told that tadpoles will grow to an enormous size in the dark, but will not be transformed into frogs, except they are brought into the light. As with tadpoles, so with the animal man — it requires the light of divine life to produce its likeness.

Regeneration is a thing of degrees in the scale of development. Creeds are shells of truth — the necessary incrustations in the process of unfoldment.

It is said that a lobster changes his shell twenty-one times before he is matured; that he goes into retirement, becomes poor and pliant, before he can extricate himself. As with lobsters, so with men; it illustrates the state, the condition, we call repentance. Some of us were born so small that we must pass through similar experiences.

Crustaceans do not, in a good sense of the term, even respect each other; the larger of the same species often devour the smaller; "they love the brethren." Mr. Rynser Jones relates that he had, on one occasion, introduced six crabs of different size into an aquarium; one of them, venturing towards the middle of the reservoir, was immediately accosted by another a little larger, which took it with its claws as it might have taken a biscuit, and set about breaking its shell, and so found a way to its flesh. It dug its crooked claws into it with voluptuous enjoyment, appearing to pay no attention to the anger and jealousy of another of its companions, which was still stronger, and as cruel, and advanced towards them. But, as Horace says — and he was not the first to say it — "No one is altogether happy in this lower world." Our ferocious crustacean quietly continued its repast, when its companion seized it exactly as it had seized its prey, broke and tore it in the same fashion, penetrating to its middle, and tearing out its entrails in the same savage manner. In the meantime the victim, singularly enough, did not disturb itself for an instant, but continued to eat the first crab bit by bit, until it was itself entirely torn to pieces by its own executioner — a remarkable instance at once of insensibility to pain and of cruel infliction under the *lep talionis*. To eat and to be eaten seems to be one of the great laws of animal nature.

It is a beautiful illustration of the workings of the law of love, in commerce as well as in what is called Christianity, upon the animal plane. In the first stage it is the law of fear and force — the blood of bulls and goats; in the second stage it is the law of love in the heart — the affections, the blood of Jesus; in the third stage — the new dispensation — it is the love of genuine goodness shed abroad in the heart, the love and the affections, as well as in the head — the intellect, the upper standing, which enables the soul, through the regenerated capacities of its divine nature, to walk with God in the paths of peace.

The reason why so few of the intelligent, the refined, cultivated, and scholarly of to-day are not Christians, or being converted to Christianity, is not so much because of the inconsistencies of professors, the incapacity, worldly-mindedness, love of show, and genteel appointments of the clergy, as it is the simplicity of the theories upon which they pride themselves. It is a simplicity which, from an intelligent or creative standpoint, is foolish, idle, incompetent, unavailing, and to the same time extremely dogmatic. The intelligence of the community has outgrown all such folly as is taught in the pulpit cant of to-day.

The theories, schemes, and dogmas that served the purposes of infantile humanity will not satisfy the intellectual conditions which the use of steam and electricity have unfolded in the thinking people of to-day.

All men, in their inmost nature, love the good,

the true, and the right. "Break your pitchers, show your light," and the minions of darkness will flee before you as mist before the rising sun.

OLD AND NEW.

On sometimes gleams upon our sight,
Through present wrong, the eternal Right;
And step by step, since time began,
We see the steady gain of man.

That all of good the past hath had
Remains to make our own time glad,
Our common, daily life divine,
And every land a Palestine.

Through the harsh noises of our day,
A low, sweet prelude finds its way;
Through clouds of doubt, and creeds of fear,
A light is breaking calm and clear.

Henceforth my heart shall sigh no more
For olden time and holier store:
God's love and blessing, then and there,
Are now and here and everywhere.

—J. G. WHITTIER.

ARTICLE VIII.

LOVE OPPOSED TO BONDAGE — THE TRULY GOOD MAN — A "SWEET SINNER" AND A "SOUR SAINT," AND THE REMEDY FOR THEIR TROUBLES.

We cannot love a mere abstraction, an impalpable something; we must have an incarnation, to be efficient — the form must be our own, — our highest ideal of goodness and truth, — the Spirit the unfolding word.

Religion is its manifestation; in this sense it is opposed to bondage, as indicated in spheres below, where warfare is carried on. The leaven has done its work, the kingdom which was within, is without; it is unfolded all around and about us. To the truly good man, there is no contention or strife, no disagreeable self-denial; he puts himself in the other's place, and has no selfish self to contend with or deny. He knows the truth by being true; he reflects God by being godlike. He is a divine magnet, — he is attracted to, and attracts; he is like a chronometer, — unaffected by the external conditions in which he is placed. He knows it is the sun in the heavens that keeps the time; he is its record. He knows the fruit of the Spirit to be love, joy, and peace. He believes in a perfect Providence, a divine Husbandman; and drinks, at the fountain of gardens, the well of living water, and streams of Lebanon. Is physical or moral war, pestilence, and famine abroad in the land, threatening the destruction of Church and State? He hears the still small voice of the Father saying, "It is I; be not afraid." Does poverty stare him in the face? "He doeth all things well;" no doubt can enter there. Is sickness his portion? With countenance beaming with gladness, he exclaims, "Thou makest all my bed in sickness." Are friends taken from him? Looking to the "city which hath foundations, whose Maker and Builder is God," he sings with renewed interest, "I'm going home;" and rejoices in the hope of an eternity which knows no parting, where sin and sorrow trouble not, "for God shall wipe away all tears from their eyes," "and there shall be no more death, neither sorrow nor crying; neither shall there be any more pain; for the former things are passed away."

The good man, who walks with God, cannot have any enemies; there is no condition for enmity, or cause for enmity in him; it is only when he descends into the border states, the guerilla department of his nature, that he is persecuted, despised, and condemned; the allegorical fig-tree was not condemned for not bearing fruit out of its season, but for being out of season. No man is persecuted in these times because of his goodness; it is the difference between his profession and his practice, the inconsistencies of his life; it is the ignorant, superstitious, hypocritical, and dogmatic manner in which he persists in his course, and contends with men of straw, that produces persecution. In reality, the persecution is entirely within and of himself; all of us in that plane of life must fight it out, or go up higher.

A "sweet sinner" is more to be preferred as a friend and companion than a "sour saint"—he may be moved in the right direction; but as for a sour, vindictive saint, he had better go into retirement, as illustrated by the crustaceans, than to stand where he is, and not go anywhere. He has buried his talent in the earth, not necessarily by digging a hole in the ground, — possibly by writing creeds and canonicals, and preaching; making converts to schemes of salvation as idle as the whistling wind, possibly by speculating in stocks, trying to corner the necessities of life, which shrink and shrivel the spiritual capacities of the soul, in contradistinction to speculations in goodness and truth; which free the gold of godliness from the dust of earth, and lift the soul to God. We would not caricature or condemn the literal church. We would use the truth as a "skilful gardener would use a sharp knife to cut the bark of a hide-bound tree, and give its trunk a chance to grow."

Many an honest, self-sacrificing, devoted soul is on the dark side of Nature — in darkness, and, like owls, sees best in the night. Their light is darkness, and their day night; and though it may cause weeping, wailing, and gnashing of teeth, the angel of mercy must take from them what religion they have, in order that they may extricate themselves, or be extricated, from their present condition, in accordance with the law of love implanted within them.

ARTICLE IX.

TEACHINGS OF JESUS — VICARIOUS ATONEMENT — THE MURDERER ON THE GALLOWS — LOVE OF JESUS — THE INFERNAL ABODE, AND THE GLORY OF GOD IN THE REGENERATION OF MAN.

We speak in accordance with the teachings of Jesus; if we are guilty in one point, we are guilty in all; in other words, if we are in the sphere of selfishness, the Mosaic dispensation, or the Adamic, which is below it, we are accountable for all the misdemeanors, maltransactions, and crimes in those spheres, or the one to which we belong, and must take our proportion of penalty, which is medicinal in its action, upon and through the sphere in which it has occasion to act.

The blood of the Son of God, much less the blood of bulls and goats, can avail us nothing, except and in so far as it serves the purpose of opening up the "way, the truth, and the life," which is love (and not blood), which lifts the soul to God, and unfolds His divine presence.

The doctrine of vicarious atonement, as taught, is a maltreatment of the truth, which we will not stop here to illustrate or discuss. That we suffer each for the other, and all for the good of the race, is a fact not to be denied; but the divine chancery, the man-conceived bankrupt act, which makes paupers of us all, without inciting conditions or unfolding motives worthy of a better end, is contemptible in the extreme, and should be buried with the dead. What we need, and what the doctrine of atonement, properly inculcated, is designed to unfold, is a love for genuine goodness, which the wayfaring man, though a fool, so far as external education is concerned, may understand, and without which repentance is of little avail.

The murderer on the gallows is but the full-grown fruit, the natural product of selfishness upon the animal plane; circumstances over which we have but little control may not have placed us there, but there is a sense in which all of us that are on the animal plane in the disputed territory, conducting guerilla warfares in the spirit, if not in the letter, stand in murderers' shoes. This same love, so terrible in its effect in this stage of nature, if properly treated, would unfold the truth, — it would enlighten and transform the children of men into sons of God.

It is said that in the old schools the masters used frogs to produce certain electric effects; they gave no good reason why they did it, but continued to do so, affirming that it was the only way the thing could be done. It was not until long after, a young student had demonstrated the fact that damp paper served a better purpose, and was much easier managed, that his teaching was adopted, and came into use. What serves the purpose of progress in one age, hinders and obstructs in another. The doctrine of vicarious atonement is a frog that has served its purpose, not only as a frog, but as a tadpole; in the Mosaic as well as in the Christian Church.

This pious cant about the love we have for our blessed Jesus, when taken in contrast with our treatment of men as exhibited in what is called Christian trade and commerce, is too thin; no gold-beater ever pounded the like; it is an admixture of love to God, the divine Father, and love to our lowest animal self, which in its unsettled condition we call hell; it is a necessary state, a productive condition, that serves the purpose of divine economy. All the different departments of the infernal abode are useful, and productive of good, but it is useless to attempt to establish the Church of God, or even keep a comfortable hotel, in that department of nature. The heavens and hells are essential; no man, however well he has surveyed the territory, can draw an exact dividing line between them: they mix and blend like the colors of the rainbow; they shoot up and reflect like the northern lights; they are as inseparably connected as the sovereignty of God and the agency of man. In short, it is the duality of nature, which, like the poles, act and react upon each other.

The pure in heart see God; no absolute evil, no human soul, is utterly incorrigible to them; all things serve the purpose of the divine will.

The meek inherit the earth; they have left the animal plane of thought, motive, and action, as we leave squeezed lemons and oranges. The good all extracted, they have skimmed the cream from off the milk of human kindness, condensed, solidified, and crystallized it here on earth, in the fire of love, so as to reflect the glory of God in the regeneration of man.

THE APOSTOLATE OF MAN.

Hearts of love and souls of daring, in the world's high field of action,
Ye who cherish God's commandments, bending not to rank or faction:
Ye whose life in slothful pleasure never sinks nor idly stagnates,
Ye who wield the scales of justice, weighing peasant men with magnates,
Lo! the voice of benediction falls upon you from on high:
Ye are chosen, ye are missioned, ye are watched by heaven's eye!

Ye have voices, thought, and feelings, they were given by God to bless you:
Pour them forth, till tyrants hear you, till they fear you, and redress you;
Ye have friends in all God's servants, friends in heaven with power supernal,
Friends in all who worship justice, all who fear the great eternal:
Raise your voices from the Forum, challenge wrong upon its throne,
Let your avalanchine warnings sweep the earth from zone to zone!

*   *   *   *   *

Speak to kings, like Paul to Festus, till they own the truths ye teach them;
Speak to men like Christ to Lazarus, till the breath of life shall reach them;
Though ye lie like Paul, in fetters, angel hands shall ope your prison:
Though ye die, as died the Prophets, trust ye still, your prayers have risen!
Pause not! fear not, bold reformers! grapple still each human ban!
Ye are prophets of the future, the Apostolate of Man!

— DUGANNE.

ARTICLE X.

THE CHRISTIAN RELIGION — JOSEPH'S COAT — CHRISTIANITY FROM AN INTELLECTUAL STANDPOINT — RELIGIOUS PERSECUTION — INGERSOLL IN SEARCH OF THE GODS, AND THE WORK HE IS DOING.

The Christian religion, as understood, taught, and practised in the literal church, is a failure, except as means to ends.

It is a worn-out garment unbecoming the age in which we live — a sort of "linsey-woolsey" patchwork, that has begun to come apart. Allegorically speaking, it is the Joseph's coat of many colors, dipped in blood (it is the coat we are describing, and not the Joseph that was sold into Egypt). Each denomination of Christendom is a patch that distorts and obscures the truth which underlies and seeks expression in the various denominational garbs assumed.

Christianity, from an intellectual standpoint,

consists and includes not only the teachings of Jesus — the apostles, the fathers of the Church, but also the creeds and practices of the Christian churches and Christian nations throughout the world. As such, it is as much a matter of history to be decided upon in regard to its merit and authority, as anything else.

I quote largely from Ingersoll (supplying the words in italic), an able exponent on the external plane, in search of the gods. He is a noble fellow, doing a good work. To say the least, he is ready to do it when the time comes; in fact, it is in part from reading his Oration on the Gods that I have been induced to publish this brief compendium of what the Christ really is — what its teachings really are. He says, in the conclusion of his work:

"Religious persecution springs from a due admixture of love towards God and hatred towards man.

"The terrible religious wars that inundated the world with blood tended, at least, to bring all religion into disgrace and hatred. Thoughtful people began to question the divine origin of a religion that made its believers hold the rights of others in absolute contempt. A few began to compare Christianity with the religions of heathen people, and were forced to admit that the difference was hardly worth dying for. They also found that other nations were even happier and more prosperous than their own. They began to suspect that their religion, after all, was not of much real value.

"For three hundred years the Christian world endeavored to rescue from the 'Infidel' the empty sepulchre of Christ. For three hundred years the armies of the Cross were baffled and beaten by the victorious hosts of an impudent impostor. This immense fact sowed the seeds of distrust throughout all Christendom, and millions began to lose confidence in a God who had been vanquished by Mohammed. The people also found that commerce made friends where religion made enemies, and that religious zeal was utterly incompatible with peace between nations or individuals. They discovered that those who loved the gods most were apt to love men least; that the arrogance of universal forgiveness was amazing; that the most malicious had the effrontery to pray for their enemies, and that humility and tyranny were the fruit of the same tree.

"For ages a deadly conflict has been waged between a few brave men and women of thought and genius upon the one side, and the great ignorant religious mass on the other. This is the war between Science and Faith. The few have appealed to reason, to honor, to law, to freedom, to the known, and to happiness here in this world. The many have appealed to prejudice, to fear, to miracle, to slavery, to the unknown, and to misery hereafter. The few have said, 'Think!' The many have said, 'Believe!'

"The first doubt was the womb and cradle of progress, and, from the first doubt, man has continued to advance. Men began to investigate, and the church began to oppose. The astronomer scanned the heavens, while the church branded his grand forehead with the word 'Infidel,' and now, not a glittering star in all the vast expanse bears a Christian name. In spite of all religion, the geologist penetrated the earth, read her history in books of stone, and found, hidden within her bosom, souvenirs of all the ages. Old ideas perished in the retort of the chemist, and useful truths took their places. One by one religious conceptions have been placed in the crucible of science, and thus far nothing but dross has been found. A new world has been discovered by the microscope; everywhere has been found the infinite; in every direction man has investigated and explored, and nowhere, in earth or stars, has been found the footstep of any being superior to, or independent of, nature. Nowhere has been discovered the slightest evidence of any interference from without; *it must come from within.*

"These are the sublime truths that enabled man to throw off the yoke of superstition. These are the splendid facts that snatched the sceptre of authority from the hands of priests.

"In that vast cemetery, called the past, are most of the religions of men, and there, too, are nearly all their gods. The sacred temples of India were ruins long ago. Over column and cornice; over the painted and pictured walls cling and creep the trailing vines. Brahma, the golden, with four heads and four arms; Vishnu, the sombre, the punisher of the wicked, with his three eyes, his crescent, and his necklace of skulls; Siva, the destroyer, red with seas of blood; Kali, the goddess; Draupadi, the white-armed, and Crishna, the Christ, *of unfolding nature*, all passed away and left the thrones of heaven desolate. Along the banks of the sacred Nile, Isis no longer wandering weeps, searching for the dead Osiris. The shadow of Typhon's scowl falls no more upon the waves. The sun rises as of yore, and his golden beams still smite the lips of Memnon, but Memnon is as voiceless as the Sphinx. The sacred fanes are lost in desert sands; the dusty mummies are still waiting for the resurrection promised by their priests, and the old beliefs, wrought in curiously sculptured stone, sleep in the mystery of a language lost and dead. Odin, the author of life and soul, Vili and Ve, and the mighty giant Ymir, strode long ago from the icy halls of the North; and Thor, with iron glove and glittering hammer, dashes mountains to the earth no more. Broken are the circles and cromlechs of the ancient Druids; fallen upon the summits of the hills, and covered with the centuries' moss, are the sacred cairns. The divine fires of Persia and of the Aztecs have died out in the ashes of the past, and there is none to rekindle, and none to feed, the holy flames. The harp of Orpheus is still; the drained cup of Bacchus has been thrown aside; Venus lies dead in stone, and her white bosom heaves no more with love. The streams still murmur, but no naiads bathe; the trees still wave, but in the forest aisles no dryads dance. The gods have flown from high Olympus. Not even the beautiful women can lure them back, and even Danæ lies unnoticed, naked to the stars. Hushed forever are the thunders of Sinai; lost are the voices of the prophets, and the land, once flowing with milk and honey, is but a desert waste. One by one the myths have faded from the clouds; one by one the phantom host has disappeared, and one by one, facts, truths and realities have taken their places. The supernatural has almost gone, but the natural remains. The gods have fled, but man is here.

"'Nations, like individuals, have their periods of youth, of manhood and decay.' Religions are the same. The same inexorable destiny awaits them all. The gods, created by the nations, must perish with their creators. They were created by men, and, like men, they must pass away. The deities of one age are the by-words of the next. The religion of our day and country is no more exempt from the sneer of the future than the others have been. When India was supreme, Brahma sat upon the world's throne. When the sceptre passed to Egypt, Isis and Osiris received the homage of mankind. Greece, with her fierce valor, swept to empire, and Jove put on the purple of authority. The earth trembled with the tread of Rome's intrepid sons, and Jupiter grasped with mailed hand the thunderbolts of heaven. Rome fell, and Christians from her territory, with the red sword of war, carved out the ruling nations of the world, and now Christ sits upon the old throne. Who will be his successor?

"Day by day religious conceptions grow less and less intense. Day by day the old spirit dies out of book and creed. The burning enthusiasm, the quenchless zeal of the early church have gone, never, never to return. The ceremonies remain, but the ancient faith is fading out of the human heart. The worn-out arguments fail to convince, and denunciations that once blanched the faces of a race, excite in us only derision and disgust. As time rolls on the miracles grow mean and small, and the evidences our fathers thought conclusive utterly fail to satisfy us. There is an 'irrepressible conflict' between *external* religion and science, and they cannot peaceably occupy the same brain nor the same world. *Christianity must come forth and show itself upon a higher plane.*

"While utterly discarding all creeds, and denying the truth of all religions, there is neither in my heart nor upon my lips a sneer for the hopeful, loving and tender souls who believe that from all this discord will result a perfect harmony; that every evil will in some mysterious way become a good, and that above and over all there is a being who, in some way, will reclaim and glorify every one of the children of men; but for the creeds of those who glibly prove that salvation is almost impossible; that damnation is almost certain; that the highway of the universe leads to hell; who fill life with fear, and death with horror; who curse the cradle and mock the tomb, it is impossible to entertain other than feelings of pity, contempt and scorn.

"Reason, Observation and Experience — the Holy Trinity of Science — have taught us that happiness is the only good; that the time to be happy is now, and the way to be happy is to make others so. This is enough for us. In this belief we are content to live and die. If, by any possibility, the existence of a power superior to, and independent of, nature shall be demonstrated, there will then be time enough to kneel. Until then, let us stand erect.

"Notwithstanding the fact that infidels in all ages have battled for the rights of man, and have at all times been the fearless advocates of liberty and justice, we are constantly charged by the church with tearing down without building again. The church should by this time know that it is utterly impossible to rob men of their opinions. The history of religious persecution fully establishes the fact that the mind necessarily resists and defies every attempt to control it by violence. The mind necessarily clings to old ideas until prepared for the new. The moment we comprehend the truth, *as it was in Jesus*, all erroneous ideas are of necessity cast aside.

"A surgeon once called upon a poor cripple and kindly offered to render him any assistance in his power. The surgeon began to discourse very learnedly upon the nature and origin of disease; of the curative properties of certain medicines; of the advantages of exercise, air and light, and of the various ways in which health and strength could be restored. These remarks were so full of good sense, and discovered so much profound thought and accurate knowledge, that the cripple, becoming thoroughly alarmed, cried out, 'Do not, I pray you, take away my crutches. They are my only support, and without them I should be miserable indeed!' 'I am not going,' said the surgeon, 'to take away your crutches. I am going to cure you, and then you will throw the crutches away yourself.'

"For the vagaries of the clouds the infidels proprose to substitute the realities of earth; for superstition, the splendid demonstrations and achievements of science; and for theological tyranny, the chainless liberty of thought.

"We do not say that we have discovered all; that our doctrines are the all in all of truth. We know of no end to the development of man. We cannot unravel the infinite complications of matter and force. The history of one monad is as unknown as that of the universe; one drop of water is as wonderful as all the seas; one leaf as all the forests; and one grain of sand as all the stars.

"We are not endeavoring to chain the future,

but to free the present. We are not forging fetters for our children, but we are breaking those our fathers made for us. We are the advocates of inquiry, of investigation and thought. This of itself is an admission that we are not perfectly satisfied with all our conclusions. Philosophy has not the egotism of faith. While superstition builds walls and creates obstructions, science opens all the highways of thought. We do not pretend to have circumnavigated everything, and to have solved all difficulties, but we do believe that it is better to love men than to fear gods; that it is grander and nobler to think and investigate for yourself than to repeat a creed, or quote Scripture like a religious parrot, with the countenance of a dyspeptic owl. We are satisfied that there can be but little liberty on earth while men worship a tyrant in heaven. We do not expect to accomplish everything in our day; but we want to do what good we can, and to render all the service possible in the holy cause of human progress. We know that doing away with gods and supernatural persons and powers is not at an end. It is a means to an end; the real end being the happiness of man.

"Felling forests is not the end of agriculture.

Driving pirates from the sea is not all there is of commerce.

"We are laying the foundations of the grand temple of the future — not the temple of all the gods, but of all the people — wherein, with appropriate rites, will be celebrated the religion of Humanity. We are doing what little we can to hasten the coming of the day when society shall cease producing millionaires and mendicants — gorged indolence and famished industry — truth in rags, and superstition robed and crowned. We are looking for the time when the useful shall be the honorable; when the true shall be the beautiful, and when REASON, throned upon the world's brain, shall be the King of kings and God of gods."

"LET there be Light! said God;
And o'er the blooming sod
Broke forth the Morn!
Glad nature smiled in mirth,
While beauty filled the earth,
And flowers were born!"

ARTICLE XI.

CHRISTIANITY NOT A FAILURE — THE LAW OF LIFE — THE FIRST AND SECOND COMING OF THE CHRIST — PRAYER ILLUSTRATED — THE CONDITION OF OUR COUNTRY — WHAT IS RECOMMENDED — WHAT SHOULD BE DONE, AND HOW TO DO IT — OUR FINAL HOME.

Light dawns upon the world; where we stand, the sun does not really shine, but stars reflect its light, and flowers are born. The so-called infidel and sceptic are doing their part to awake and unfold the day. Christianity, as understood and practised in Church and State, throughout Christendom, is a misnomer; the time is at hand when it will be as difficult to find a fighting Christian, a contentious stickler for creed or canonical, as it is to find a white blackbird.

Christianity, properly understood, is no failure. Those of us who think it is, have only seen the sign of Jonah — the great fish — the stable, and not the church, in which the Christ is born —

the Joseph's coat — the grave in which the allegorical Lazarus sleepeth.

We are familiar with the literal betrayal, crucifixion, and entombment of Jesus, in whom the Christ obtained; but so far as its spiritual resurrection in our hearts and consciences is concerned, many of us have not even heard. Possibly we have only seen the husks of truth upon which swine are fed, not even the interior shell, to say nothing of the meat — the life-giving substance within. The Christ of Christianity is not dependent upon the Bible, the teachings of Jesus, the Apostles, the Fathers of the Church, or the creeds that have preceded us; they may not be adapted to our states and conditions. The Christ is the unfolding — the infallible word — the Bible-maker adapted to all states and conditions of men. What we need, and what we must have, in order to be saved, in a good sense of that term, is an infallible interpreter; in short, the opening up within our consciousness of the Christ, that shall be, unto us human souls, what instinct is to the animal kingdom — the controlling power that directs all its actions. The mistake we have made, has been in attempting to establish the kingdom of heaven upon the animal plane.

As the monkey and the ape, as well as the lion and the lamb, preceded us in the order of creation, so the external forms and teachings of Christianity preceded and made possible the more spiritual and perfect, which is now in order. "Listen that ye may hear, seek that ye may find, knock that it may be opened up unto you."

The allegorical serpent in the Garden of Eden was the Christ of nature; it beguiled, that it might unfold a higher life; it was God's mode of operation. It tempted Jesus in the wilderness, that it might unfold the way. The an-hungeredment was in that direction; it forsook its external self in the crucifixion, that it might reveal the truth. It reorganized the external particles of its spiritual body, that it might demonstrate its life, its transforming power, on matter as well as on mind. The allegorical serpent in the garden represents the unprogressed, the unregenerated soul of man. In other words, the Christ in the unregenerate soul is a serpent. Regeneration transforms itself into the dove of divine life.

Temptation is the going out through some department of our affectional nature after the cause which moved the soul to act. It supposes desire and an opportunity to gratify it. It is a response to the law of love. Every soul not absolutely good is liable to temptation. The more perfect or progressed the soul, the more spiritual or refined the tempter. Our safety lies in our dependence upon the God within; hence the prayer, "Lead us not into temptation, but deliver us from evil," etc. The motives which actuate us when we yield to temptation, are not the result of spiritual contemplations. In such cases we do not pause to look deep down in the fount of life. Had we done so, the immediate cause which moved us to act would have lost its power to control. Love would have risen above the sediment of our animal nature, and we might have been repelled and restrained from the comparative evil, by the divinity which enlightens our consciences and shapes our ends.

Love, which is the cause of spiritual illumination, is free. It comes welling up in the hearts and consciences of harmonious souls, from the divine within, like water in a literal well. It flows into the soul, and through its affectional nature, from the fountain of life, in accordance with law. Temptation is a means through which the unfolding spirit is enabled to receive spiritual emanations of truth from each, and impart to all. The law through which this is done is eternal, and cannot be broken or rendered inactive. What we call sin, or the transgression of the law, is obedience to that same law in its more external spheres of being. When we consider that love in the animal is blind, that its degree of spiritual development has not unfolded an individualized consciousness of a better or best state and capacity, we see the use of temptation — that it is an appointed means to unfold a freedom of the affections which, under God and his providences, must ultimate perfection in the human soul.

Each step we take as we journey home to God is a degree in the spheres of good and use. As we journey through the discrete orders of love, we leave behind, as dead and worthless, those things which once allured us outward and upward in life. The things which once tempted us have lost their power.

The present discordant conditions of the religious world demand reformations calculated to develop the spiritual capacities of the soul. Organizations, as means to ends, is in harmony with nature — it is God's mode of operation; we see it in every department of life; every living thing furnishes an illustration. Each human soul is an organized power, more or less advanced as an instrumentality in the process of unfolding — a conscious individual receptacle of divine life in the great humanitary man. The first dispensation is doing its work. It has shaken external religion from its centre; its cardinal dogmas are surrendered as uncertain or provisional; its intellectual framework has given way. The repose, the unity, the permanency of the literal Church has gone forever. The unguided feelings and fluctuations of moral conception take their place in continued agitation and strife. They cannot organize, construct, and bring order out of the intellectual anarchy which prevails. This stage of development is the Samson among the Philistines. It has hold of our dual nature. The house divided against itself must come down. The tablets of stone which contain the Commandments written within the soul by the finger of God, must be smitten; the fountains of the mighty deep must be broken up, so that light, love, and life may flow from the within, enlightening and inspiring the progressive soul to discover and occupy the spiritual temple — the house not made with hands, which cannot be destroyed. The present discordant conditions demand new designs fresh from the foundries of heaven, the creative spheres — the key-boards of creation — so conditioned that the sons of God can play upon the organs of life, adapting each part of our compound and complex body to all other parts, bringing the whole into an attuned at-one-ment, thus creatively unfolding the *word* — the kingdom within. The supply of such a demand necessarily unfolds the Christ, the quickening spirit which destroys the old, and has power to construct the new, to reveal the eternal.

The new Jerusalem — the sea of glass — is a universal necessity. The Christ of Christianity demands a new government, a theocracy begotten in the hearts and consciences of all mankind, the original and supreme love so conceived and conditioned as to demonstrate in earth-life the gospel of peace and good-will to all mankind. Then, and not till then, will war cease, and charity, or spiritual non-resistance, be possible to all men.

Spiritual demands causatively create spiritual supplies. It is difficult to determine which is first, the demand or the supply. It seems like the discovery of truth in the Word, to have existed before it was born. While the unfolding child is being developed to make the demand, the supply is being unfolded to satisfy the demand when made. The Christ which preëminently obtained in Jesus has long since gone to the Spiritual Universe, the Father's house of many mansions, to prepare a supply. The coming man has literally rapped at the door of our understanding, and now waits at the gate of life, that he may enter, organize, and supply all our spiritual needs. The needs of the nineteenth century demand a theocracy, a union of states in love and affection, a blending of harmonious souls in intimate communion with God, so that the loves, desires, and interests of each can expressively reflect the good of all as it exists in the Divine Father. Such a union of spiritual states and governments would abolish all the evils of life without enacting or abolishing a single law.

Attraction and repulsion seem to be the means through which the Creator unfolds Himself in the works of creation.

The law of love pervades every department of Nature. It is God's mode of operation. "God is love." Mind and matter, like cause and effect, are inseparably connected. Each expression of life, each partly progressed effect in the mineral and the vegetable as well as in the animal kingdom, is true to itself, the spirit or God-power which provides and controls in its sphere of activity. In the more external manifestations of life in which the lawgiver has not obtained a harmonious expression, the law seems to clash. Were it not for the fact that the centrifugal and centripetal forces balance each other, or are balanced in love, the soul of the universe, the great humanitary man, would fly asunder and be destroyed. Were it not for the fact that the inner love — the Omnipresent law — overrules and controls all the departments of life, individual sovereignty would be a curse! Were it not for the fact that the exercise of what little sovereignty or freedom of affection we at present - possess, was the only means of obtaining a more perfected state, we might question the propriety of its exercise; as it is, we feel that there are goods and uses that we have little or no conception of. We perceive what to us constitutes the good, the better, and the best. We know by experience (it constitutes the sum and substance of our religion) that we are bound by the law of God through which he is reproducing himself in us.

It is impossible to study Nature with a spiritual desire to discover the purest beauty, the truest good, without unfolding the Divine within. It is the law of life — the result of attraction, temptation, and repulsion. The different spheres of good and use which the unfolding soul learns by experience, as it journeys home to God, satisfies the traveller that there is an internal department of his nature in which the Infinite Spirit is enthroned in love. It is by passing through the discrete orders of love, that we perceive the uses of war and all the comparative evils which self-love and blind passions have projected upon the race. It is not until or only in proportion as we learn their good or use that the soul is saved, or past their need. There is no salvation from evil within its sphere. The exercise of our affections in the plane which we occupy is destined to project us above it. It is the only means by which we may obtain the good we need. Temptation is a good; it has a use, it is the divinely-appointed way through which the Creator unfolds His creation. It has been said, "Covet earnestly the best gifts"; it is right so to do, but there is a better way. It is called charity — a quality of love, or state of the affections, which finds its true affinity within itself, the holiest of the holy; the Christ, or Lamb of God, which taketh away the sins of the world by lifting us above it.

Our experience and observation in Christianity leads us to the conclusion that we, images of the Almighty, upon whom we are dependent for inspiration to understand and be instructed in spiritual realities, ought not to expect very spiritual communications, or much satisfaction in spiritual communion, until the spiritual desire is more fully awakened within us. "We must be born again;" and not only so, but again and again we must be transformed by the renewing of our spiritual affections, as we pass up, step by step, toward the top of the mount where everything that is, is true and *right*. I am satisfied that in our Father's house, the spiritual universe, there are many mansions, occupied by mediatorial minds, through which each soul born of the spirit, or in the affection of good and truth, may go or be drawn in accordance with the law of love into the very presence-chamber of the Almighty, where love absolute and eternal is so expressed as to render and adapt itself — its good — its use, unto all conditions of being.

We believe it may be possible for all in the spheres of charity to so blend their spiritual aspirations as to move the Almighty, causing love to flow through the understanding in such a manner that error, discord, or deception regarding the way of life, would be impossible. We believe in spiritual realities; that the spiritual universe is within the material, and is its constructive apartment, which has within it the divine essence or creative power to fashion substance in its own image, through which it unfolds and reflects itself in proportion to the degree of spirituality obtained. We are satisfied that there are many lost or unfound conditions of soul in the spiritual universe, as yet unoccupied departments in our Father's house, except by the unborn sons, which exist as essence in the bosom of the Father.

All such unfound or discordant conditions of being, which in the affection of evil, delight in mischief, malice, and war — incorrigible and useless as they seem to be, have their origin in good; and though separated from it by impassable gulfs of unattuned love and affection, are and must remain (so long as incorrigible) necessities as means to ends, stepping-places in the eternal standing stool of law, which, under God, is our schoolmaster pricking and paining us, except we stand erect. We believe that the mind, the inherent life or spirit in matter, is one and the same thing in all human souls, and that the difference in manifestation is the result of peculiar individualization, brought about by the providences of God, through which each soul, not finally incorrigible, obtains the same essential elements, differently proportioned, combined, and conditioned. These differences, which, under God, unfold the dynamics, rhythm, and gamut of life, will enable each soul, when voiced in harmony with the celestial, to understandingly perform its part in the anthem of life. Some are so harmoniously unfolded and spiritual in their tendencies, that spiritual love, light, and life flow from or through them to bless, reform, and beautify all who come within their sphere; they bring the balm from Gilead — the essence of goodness — its oil and wine, which, being poured into wounded souls, unfolds the tree of life in the garden of the Lord.

Condition ourselves as best we can, it seems difficult, if not impossible, at all times, to produce a perfect control of our animal self; and, so long as selfishness is in us, error, if not deception, is liable to manifest itself. We have found but few, if any, that we could feel were the mouth of God speaking His infallible word to our souls. We have found it necessary to go, and go alone, beyond the "watchman upon the walls of Zion," if we would see and know the truth. Books and teachers serve as helps. We have found by experience that error sometimes serves the purpose. They have served a purpose in all the religions of the past. In the consideration of this question, and all questions pertaining to the subject, much depends upon the definition we give to terms used. There is a sense in which we accept each circumstance and phenomenon of life as a special manifestation of God in His providences; and in doing this, we define truth to be the best expression the absolute Being could obtain in the sphere of activity through which He is speaking. From this standpoint we accept everything said as true to the condition which produced its utterance. The soul which actually occupies this position, and lives the life of trust, lives in the continual enjoyment of a peaceful flow of love and good-will from God to all mankind. To such a soul, the incongruities and discrepancies which tempt the merely intellectual man to disbelieve in spiritual realities and in a personal God, who creates or fashions substance, and takes note of heart-states, and knows and supplies the requirements of each, do not exist. Faith in the God which "does not quench the smoking flax or break the bruised reed," begets hope in His immediate and direct action through receptive instrumentalities. Such a belief, faith and hope, enable the believer to so purify his affections as to see the Creator in the works of creation; to hear His voice and feel His presence in the most discordant and contentious circles, saying, "It is I; be not afraid." Such experiences unfold the spiritual capacities of the soul, and resolve its desires into an attuned at-one-ment with the purest good and truest use, in such a manner as to unfold its presence, saying, "Peace, be still. Come up higher."

God breathes into man the breath of life, and he becomes a living soul. The Almighty enlightens his understanding, and he becomes a quickened spirit. We have thought that the human soul, in its essential, its spiritual part, is a reproduction of the divine — the production of its interior self, the Christ; that this was done through receptive instrumentalities, in such a manner as to create individual responsibilities and capacities, to enjoy without multiplying the godhead, increasing spirit, or creating matter; that inspiration, and the change called death, which is continually going on in every living soul, were the means through which it was performed; that there is a sense in which God lives, moves, and has His being in every living thing. Man is a triune being. When harmoniously developed, he is the spiritual temple of the living God. It is with the spiritual as with the literal or Jewish temple — each has its outer, its inner, and inmost courts, or holiest of the holy. The one is beautifully expressive of the other. The construction, furniture, and service of the Jewish or literal temple, was not the result of blind chance, finite invention or design; it was the work of divinely inspired artists and artizans. Probably they did not perceive or comprehend the truths or principles expressed in the model made, any better than we perceive or comprehend the finger of God in the phenomena of our day. It was then, with the Jewish, the literal temple, as it is now with the spiritual, the transcendental temple. God, through receptive instrumentalities, is the maker and builder thereof; He is the all in all; He inspires each and all in their different spheres of good and use. There is no devil in hell that is not executing God's designs. Each artist and artizan will receive his meat in due season.

The Bible prophets spake as they were moved; theirs was the day of types and shadows. The prophets that are to be, will speak as they perceive, in accordance with their degree of spiritual enlightenment; for the coming is to be the day of spiritual realities. The truths of the past will be understood; we shall know there is a spirit in man, and that the inspiration of the Almighty giveth him understanding. Spiritual understanding — the result of inspiration — is dependent upon spiritual activities. It is not a subject or thing to be taught; it is a condition of the soul, to be felt and known by experience; it is something that touches the sensation of the soul. The principle of inspiration is eternal; men are different, and are consequently differently affected by it. The laws through which inspiration is given are not changed, but the conditions are ever changing. Inspiration differs as men differ. There is a sense in which the Almighty gives the soul understanding, that is above the ordinary affairs of human life. The spiritual-minded, loving soul, who lives in the interior department of his being (the temple of the living God) may be inspired from the Almighty, the inmost of the within, the holiest of the holy. He may commune with the cherubims and seraphims at the altar of eternal life. The quickened spirit, the resurrected Christ, may stand forth within him, constituting an open door, the way or well of life, of which, if a man drink, he will never die. He that would come unto God, or be inspired, must believe that He is, and that He is the rewarder of all those who diligently seek and serve Him in spirit and in truth.

Christianity, properly understood, is the spiritual communion service and worship of the Infinite

Spirit, in spirit and in truth. It is the external product of its internal self. Its effects are to reflect — to extend the light of life — to unfold the spiritual temple of the living God. It includes within its communion all the servants who render service in the cause of justice, mercy and truth.

Christians believe in the Infinite Spirit — the Divine Father — and in being guided by him in communion and fellowship in the spirit. Christians, to a greater or less extent, see the light, hear the voice, and feel the presence of the spirit, but know not whence it cometh or whither it goeth.

Spirit is called an immaterial substance; it being more ethereal than the external census of the soul, it eludes our grasp. As it cannot be weighed or measured, it seems to the materialist to have neither weight nor measure, as though it did not occupy space, and was incapable of organization, extension or division. "As the soul thinketh, so is it." To the spiritually blind, who accept the literal definition, spirit is not anything but breath or wind. To such minds, what we have said, or may say, on this subject, is mere transcendental nonsense — metaphysical moonshine. We grant there is some truth as well as beauty in the exclamation of the critic: "Behold, what drivelling madmen these insane Christians — Nature's journeymen — are making of themselves." Be it so; but if we can but touch one such soul in the right spot, this moonshine will do its work. Truth, the great master-builder in Nature, which constructively unfolds the Christ, will have received another apprentice; the spiritual gate will be opened to the critic, to walk in as well as criticise. To the practical Christian, who is born of the water and of the spirit, so as to unfold the departments of his material as well as spiritual nature in the pursuit of interior good, spirits or spiritual bodies are substance — a cogitative substance imbued with instinct — perception and power to think, feel, and act, which unfolds and embodies different qualities of mind which pervade each other, and permeates all kinds of matter. In this sense, spirit or spiritual bodies occupy space — are capable of organization, extension and division, by, through, or in virtue of individualized intonations of love and affection which constitute the dynamics, rhythm and gamut of divine life. For aught we know, (and the belief is in harmony with everything known,) there are as many kinds, conditions, or qualities of spiritual substance, as there is of earth matter, material substance. Probably each is destined to unfold and ultimate itself through higher forms, to be unfolded by the Creator in his highest form of creation. Man, the human soul, being the effect of, and the culminating point, in the works of creation, necessarily embodies within himself all the elements, all the life-principles of the organized forms or soul-expressions of life which preceded him; they constitute the material and spiritual substances upon which the human soul subsists. The receptive soul receives and appropriates these elements, these partly unfolded principles of divine life, in accordance with the law of God, in its plane of development. Such an execution unfolds the divine form from within the spiritual temple, its holiest of the holy, which reforms and regenerates the human soul, causing it to bud, blossom, and embody the delicious fruit of eternal life.

Eternal life and eternal death are interchangeable terms, signifying positive and negative states which act and react upon each other, thus progressively unfolding itself, the principle, the agency implanted within. Eternal life is a continued change; eternal death is the unawakened cause of its unfoldment. We die to the old progressively as we are born to the new. The last enemy, the *old serpent* — death — is thus regeneratively transformed into the dove of divine life. To the extent we partake of the tree of knowledge, we die to the condition of ignorance. Knowledge is distinguished from wisdom, in this : that knowledge is a capacity to do, to partake of the tree of life, while wisdom is the thing done, or the cheerful unfoldment of the will to do it. The trouble with Christendom to-day is more of the heart, its affections, its will and "upper-standing," than it is of the head — the intellect. Christianity, as practised, is little else than a skin of truth, stuffed and put on like an extended bustle, which extorts and crucifies the maltreated human form.

The real thing, Christianity, opened up from within, tends to unfold, harmonize, and bless, not only the possessor, but all that comes within its sphere. The shoddy shoes and clothing furnished through the medium of Christian commerce, is a more truthful criterion to judge Christianity by than the profession it makes.

Many Christians are looking for some miraculous transitions in the affairs of life. There are many fathers and mothers in the spiritual Israel, who, like Simeon of old, desire and expect some especially divine embodiment in human form — an Israelite in thought, word, and deed, in whom there shall be no guile — that shall stand up among the people as a divine centre, clothed with authority to teach the *Christ*, to unfold the *word*, and to whom all shall gravitate. What these friends expect to see in some one man, we expect to see in all men. We see, or think we see, the Christ, the coming man, the unfolding word, the soul of the spiritual universe, coming to all men. We believe each individual soul to be divine in its internal nature, each alike central and essential; all alike sons and heirs of immortality; each a teacher to reflect, to contribute, its part through the associate soul of the spiritual universe, to unfold and embody the word, the coming man, in the hearts and consciences of the race.

We do not expect to find any individual furnished with letters patent from the Court of Heaven, granting to him or his the exclusive right to teach, reform, or organize. We do not believe that true

Religion can be taught, reformed, or organized by uninspired man. It is, or has within it, the Christ, the teacher, the reformer, which enlightens, reforms, and brings the individual through the processes of spiritualization into harmony with its interior self.

Christianity is destructive as well as constructive and creative in its effects — the Christ, or quickening spirit, comes not in its first comings to bring peace to the soul. It comes to bring the sword, to create discord, contention and strife. It divides the house against itself. The external, the animal department (in which the unregenerated man lives) is divided against its internal or spiritual, which allies to God and celestial influences. The Divine Spirit, or Christ within the holiest of the holy, is not divided; it is the fathers and mothers-in-law, and their demoniac associates, which are divided and opposed to the Divine will, and strive together for the mastery. The house thus divided cannot stand, it must be destroyed; the external or first phase must pass away. Jesus, in whom the Christ, the quickened spirit obtained, and through whom it spake, said, in exhibiting the Jewish Temple, (the model,) it shall be destroyed, there shall not be one stone left upon another, in contemplating his physical dissolution (the dispensation of blood), the destruction of the Jewish Temple (the dispensation of rights and shadows), and the end of the world (the dispensation of external authorities, creeds and canonicals) — speaking of them as one and the same thing, said, "I have power to destroy this temple and raise it again in three days." The religious world has passed through two of these dispensations: the Mosaic, that of fear and force, the literal coming of Christ, the dispensation of love — and now the Christ comes to introduce the third dispensation: that of wisdom, which is the product of an enlightened understanding that affects the hearts and consciences of men. Its work is to destroy the literal church, the external temple, the house divided against itself, and causatively construct, or creatively reveal, the broad church, the spiritual temple, as it exists in the divine mind. The dispensation of wisdom cannot dawn upon all souls at one and the same time. The coming Christ depends upon our interior capacity to perceive and comprehend; it finds us occupying different standpoints, each differently capacitated from all others, for spiritual enlightenment. We cannot see the same light, hear the same voice, or feel the same good and use, only as we arrive at like states of mental and spiritual growth. The great majority of us are still in the house of bondage, the dispensation of force and fear. Few, very few, have had those tables of stone broken within them, so that the light of love can reflect the law of the Lord as it is written within.

The actions which we condemn in ourselves and others, which many regard as a positive proof of spiritual death and moral destruction, we accept as evidence of spiritual life and future well-being; they are the external manifestations of internal and spiritual activities, and may be medicinal in their tendencies. The discordant condition most Christians pass through while in the house of bondage, and in the process of regeneration, render them exceedingly sensitive to surroundings, and liable to demoniac infections. While journeying through the wilderness *home* to the New Jerusalem, the spiritual Canaan, there awaits the unfolding soul successive trials and temptations calculated to unfold and embody light, love and life.

We do not suppose this condition can be fully

obtained while we remain in the mortal body. We know by experience and observation that dissatisfaction, unrest, and suffering, do not always depend upon our own grossness or short-comings. Such is the solidity of society, such our relations to each other in the great humanitary man, that we necessarily suffer for others, and must continue so to do until all are brought into an attuned at-one-ment with the highest good. The more refined and spiritually beautiful the soul, the more intense the agony; and long after nothing remains in the affections to tempt or respond to temptations, the soul may be so conditioned as to almost despair, and be caused to exclaim, " My God, my God, why hast thou forsaken me?"

Christianity, as defined, is not dying out; it is entombed in the rock of ages. Its truths are eternal; they are the words of the living God, which has sought and must continue to seek a perfect and still more perfected form of expression, which is limited by our capacity to hear and pronounce — to receive and express. The soul that has heard the voice, that has perceived the light, cannot remain unmoved in, or go back to the literal church.

Merely an intellectual acceptance of the facts and philosophy of Christianity, will not reform or regenerate the individual or the world; it may serve as seed for future generations, but unless the truth be received in the soil of the soul, the garden of the Lord, and spring up through the understanding, it withers away, and, so far as the individual or age is concerned, dies out. I have never known a Christian that was born of the water, (intellectual perception of the doctrine,) and of the spirit, (enlightened affection,) that went away. Who is there that ever drank of the well, or entered the way of spiritual life, that did not hunger and thirst for more, and know by experience that such hunger and thirsting was not in vain? Why should they go away? To whom should they go? Where else is the "tree of life" — the unfolding word of God?

Christianity is not dying out, it is taking deeper root in the hearts and consciences of those that accept it. There are individual souls scattered all over the country that have from internal necessities withdrawn themselves from uncongenial associations, and stand for the present as individual magnets (spiritual lightning-rods) attracting light and love from higher life, sending it forth to all aspiring souls to warm and purify the earth.

A pure theory unfolds a correct life and happy practice. Figuratively speaking, we have friends among the *ists* in all the *isms* that have obtained since Noah came out of the Ark. Some of them are good because of their religion, organization, surroundings, etc.; others are good in spite of their religion and surroundings. A hard experience has in many cases opened up the better way — the paths of peace. Those that have drawn the finest lines of metaphysical or qualitative distinctions, have, as a rule, been the most humble, self-sacrificing and devoted to what all enlightened nations accept as justice, mercy and truth. The fact that a soul makes fine distinctions between the good, better and best, and knows that it is not possible for it to do those things which others delight in doing, does not necessarily imply self-righteousness; often quite the opposite; and in many cases it evinces a debt of gratitude, springing up within, to be paid (through less fortunate souls) to the infinite Giver who guides and protects in the way of life.

We have no doubt that such souls as are shadowed forth in the characters of Abel, Enoch, Melchisedek and Jesus, may suffer, for the sins of others, far beyond our capacity to conceive; and because of such suffering, open a fount of affection, a degree of spirituality in themselves, and others, that otherwise could not have been. This is a vicarious atonement that causatively creates sons of God through the transforming power of love.

We believe we have, or may have, some control over our love — the power that attracts and is attracted. To illustrate: We have many friends, both men and women, scattered all over the country, some of them choice souls, about fit for the kingdom of heaven, without further regeneration. Such is our relation to them as unfolding effects of the same cause, that though we may not have seen them for years, we can, by coming into what we call the contemplative mood, come into their sphere and look into their affectional nature — what we call the Garden of the Lord — and obtain, in some sense, the advantage of their presence. If we find ourselves leaning toward any one of them in a sense that tempts us to worship them, or threatens the freedom of our affections, we may, by examining carefully, though sometimes we may have to look long and close, find some fault or imperfection, which saves us from idolatry, and enables us to worship God the Father, as exhibited in the congenial soul, which was the means of our temptation. If, on the other hand, we find ourselves related, in business or otherwise, to contentious and to us disagreeable persons, and are tempted to despise and shun them, we may so enter into the spheres of causation, consider their proclivities, tendencies and surroundings, so as to perceive the why and the how their better nature has not been understood, even to themselves; thus we may be enabled to reflect the light of life from the saviours above us to the souls around and beneath.

"Fighting is by nature dear to the heart of man. The men with swords and spears, with needle-guns and rifled cannon, have by no means had a monopoly of the business. The scholars, the theologians, the men of the closet, have kept up a warfare quite as extensive and energetic. To men in earnest to advance the truth, the polemical method has often seemed the natural, and indeed the only way. It destroys charity, and rouses the spirit of strife. The *odium theologicum* has passed into a proverb for bitterness.

"No religious belief ever existed among honest men that had not in it some genuine sustaining element. Every belief which has been earnestly held, has been the result of an effort toward truth; it has attained something, but has come short of much. The way to remedy the defect is to give higher truth on the same line. Instead of wrenching from men's grasp their imperfect beliefs, we are to offer them nobler. We are not to violently uproot error, but to plant beside it truth so vital that it will absorb into itself and lift into higher life the soul of inferior growth.

"Whoever would bring men into clearer light, must not content himself with a protest against old errors. He must get hold of the moral truth which gave the error its strength, and by getting deeper into the same truth, supersede the error in its stronghold.

"Calvinism, for example, will be but idly assailed by any one who has not grasped all the truth in it, and more besides. The correction of the system lies not in a denial of these principles, but in an addition to them; in the farther truth, that in the heart of this supreme God love is supreme; in the appeal, not only to men's consciences, but to their hearts.

"All the dogmatic systems, all the ecclesiastical structures, which seem to some thinkers mere absurdities and incumbrances, have grown up to meet some want of human nature. If they are imperfect, the remedy is not to tear them up, but to provide for the want in a better way.

"To men with any touch of the soldier in them, fighting for the truth is a very pleasant occupation! Serving with the truth is a different matter. The highest gift of knowledge, the prophet's inspiration, the hero's courage, find their right place only when they are used in the service of love."

The first coming of the Christ was through the love and affections; it came with a sword; its effect was war, contention, and strife. It now comes through the will and the understanding. It comes with the olive-branch, — its effect is to be love, joy, and peace.

The fatherhood of God, the motherhood of nature, and the brotherhood of man, act and react upon each other; it is the trinity of life; they, or rather it in them, is unfolding and perfecting itself in us.

Conditions are everything. "Law is a statement of conditions." Prayer is not necessarily an external speech; it does not consist in teasing, or attempting to instruct, persuade, or overaw the Almighty.

Behold the flowers of the field, the violet, the lily, and the rose; they ask in accordance with the law of life— as mustard-seed they seek growth, as leaven they work — knocking at the doors of life, and the beauties of nature are opened up unto them.

Behold the poor, wayfaring man, clothed in rags, bleeding at every pore, perishing for love, friendship, and religious associations worthy the name, — picture in your mind's eye such an individual, sick, lame, halt, and blind, not knowing his disease, that he has a father's house, a home in heaven, that there is a balm in Gilead, a physician there; enlighten his understanding, to perceive and comprehend the facts in the case, and he is instantly transformed — every part of him becomes a prayer.

Such is the condition of Christendom to-day;

it is sick, lame, halt, and blind; the human family is famishing for love, and know it not.

This country, so far as dogmatic religion is concerned, is on the downward grade. There are breakers ahead; there is an engine coming. Clear the theological track of all its rubbish, or it will be ground to powder on the threshing-floor of divine love, its *isms* and husks of truth will be blown as chaff before the wind. The swords and spears of theological controversy must be transformed into mental ploughshares and spiritual pruning-hooks. We, as a people, must unfold our spiritual natures in accordance with the law of love, or be crushed, like the allegorical worm, through the brutal power of fear and force, godward.

Some of our religious friends recommend spiking a theological sign-board on the engine. They mean well, but are wofully mistaken; if we do it, and insist upon fear and force, we shall extort and destroy ourselves. They that take the "sword must be slain by it." The proper remedy is time and common sense, the quickening of the spirit, and the inspiration of the Almighty. We would say to the watchmen upon the walls of Zion,

"Down with the breaks, and stop the running in this literal direction; abolish all sectarian laws, and have no law upon the matter of religion but the law of God, which is written in the hearts and consciences of the race." Give us a divine secularity that will unfold the holy Catholic Church as it existed in the divine mind before the foundations of this world were laid.

It matters not so much who our parents were, where we came from, or how long we have been coming, as it does what we are, and what we are to be. It matters not so much whether the divine principle comes into us, as a spiritual gift, all at once, so as to constitute an event in our life, to be recorded as a birth, or whether it comes into us in discrete degrees, as orders of creation, so long as it is there — the unfolding word — to regenerate, transform, and demonstrate its love, will, and wisdom in the hearts and consciences of the race.

No earnest student of nature can freely study any of the arts and sciences, without, sooner or later, opening up within himself the way of life, the law of harmony, intercommunion, and telegraphic communications, to and from all other earnest students interested in the same pursuits;

much less can we *freely* study religion, the science of godliness, which includes all the arts and sciences, without unfolding within ourselves the infinite master of all the schools — the soul of all science — whose love is life, whose will is law, and whose wisdom is past finding out. Such an unfolding is the coming of the Christ, the second advent, through the will and the understanding.

The *free religionist* has but one master. As is the quality of the service rendered, so is the measure of freedom enjoyed. Such an opening up of the master is the fruitage of a good old age — a well-spent life. I care not if he be young in years, as we live in experience, observation, and practice, rather than in days and weeks; he is old and honorable in the sight of God and man.

While we have been beating and bruising ourselves against the external bearers of dogmatic theology, the foundations of the broad church have been unfolded within. While we have been blindly searching for Light and Life in the depths of religious animalism, our spiritual capacities to perceive and appreciate, as well as to know and to be, have been unfolding. We have learned, by a more or less painful experience, that the hells, as well as the heavens, are eternal; that they are states and conditions — spiral stairways through which we may pass in divine order to the mansions beyond — compensated reproductions of the tree of life implanted in the soul, some before and some after, every one in his own order, each receiving his penny. The compensating principle of law will bring us all home at last.

Most of us have very insignificant ideas of home. "We have been in the habit of thinking of home as a place built by carpenters and masons, of brick and mortar, boards and shingles, laths and plaster," and decorative ornamentation; in reality, our home beyond the tide is an expectancy; it is a state and condition that fits and fills the ever-progressive longings and capacities of the human soul. Such is our home in the "undiscovered cause" which we are to discover, furnish, and occupy; it is the presence-chamber of God, the finality of the race, the embodied soul of science in the mansions of the blest.

Yes, there is a glorious prospect,
'Tis the light of life we see,
It awakes within us mortals,
Hopes of what we are to be.

ARTICLE XII.

OUR BELIEF DEFINED — TRUTH — ITS EFFECT — NATURE — GOD'S MODE OF OPERATION — THE HARMONY OF THE SPHERES — THE JOURNEY OF LIFE ILLUSTRATED — REPUTATION AND CHARACTER — DARWINISM — FREEDOM AND ITS EFFECTS.

WE believe in the eternality of the soul, its Divine origin, spiritual relations, and ineffable destiny; in the fatherhood of God, the motherhood of nature, and the brotherhood of man.

Belief is a judicious exercise of the mind. It supposes some knowledge of the subject upon which it is to decide. A well-balanced mind weighs the evidence *pro* and *con*, and turns like a pair of scales the way the evidence preponderates.

Justice is said to be blind; but belief, to be effectual, must be clear-sighted and sound in the judicial function it performs. Such a belief is purely an intellectual matter; but belief, in its best sense, is a matter of the heart as well as of the head, — it involves a cheerful coöperation in the truth perceived, an honest endeavor to obtain its good and use.

Truth, in this sense, is the incarnating movement that connects the soul with God. It unfolds the subjective world, and gives the believer an opportunity to stand outside of external existence, or rather so distinctly inside, as to produce a standing-place as well as a fulcrum through which to move the world. Mountains of ignorance are thus displaced.

Nature — God's mode of operation — is the great lifting and moving machine of the universe. It is a system of wills within a will, that engage, connect, and control all things. There are circumferential as well as central truths, corollaries of thought, purpose, and action, distinct differentialities, that make up and constitute the trinity of life, through which the fatherhood of God, the motherhood of nature, and the brotherhood of man, act and react upon and through each other, thus unfolding the love of God in the hearts of men.

There is a principle in music by which, if certain notes are struck in their proper combinations, others will respond and unfold the law of vibration — the harmony of the sphere.

It is upon this principle that the Warden of the Eternal Garden plays upon the harp of life. As in music, so in morals and religion; if properly conditioned in an attuned at-one-ment, the soul of science will strike the chord which thrills and echoes through the inmost fibres of the soul. It is divine truth — the incarnating movement which unfolds and lifts the soul to God.

In the providences of divine harmony there are discrete degrees of goods and truths, as well as different conditions and qualities of servants and service rendered, ranging from the most abject conditions of fear and force, in the Mosaic dispensation, up through the transitional conditions of life into the freedom of perfect love, in which the Christ of God transforms, regenerates, and transmutes the baser metals of our nature into pure gold.

Such is the journey of life. The allegorical father lights the way. The son carries the fuel, but is not slain. The animal for the sacrifice is entangled in the branches, and awaits the consummation of its kingdom. "Arise, let us go hence."

In the kingdom of heaven, where the pure in heart see God, and the meek inherit the earth, there is no discord, contention, or strife. The Jacob that cheated the Esau out of his birthright is transformed — the leopard has changed its spots, the Ethiopian skin is as white as snow — it is the workings of the law of regeneration, the school-master, that unfolds the Christ. The good that Jacob robbed from Esau, when a boy, he dispensed, when old, to the world — to all his children's children that may come after him. In brief, it is the glory of God in the salvation of the race.

"There is no evil in the city, and the Lord hath not done it." There is an all-pervading essence, or principle, which we believe in and call God, which exists in and permeates all matter; in a sense, to be considered its cause — its life — its unfolding word, the diadem, or crowning work, of which we, the individual gems of eternal life, can never be more than unfolding and reflecting parts.

There is in reality no new thing, or absolute spiritual progress, under the sun. God our Father is a finality, pervading and unfolding all conditions of matter. He is the one only Eternal now in which we live, move, and have the privilege of unfolding and perfecting ourselves in accordance with His law. Time, common sense, the quickening of the spirit, and the inspiration of the Almighty, will reveal it unto you. It is written in your heart — your affectional nature — the garden of the Lord — the "vineyard" of the Christ, in which every man that works shall receive his "penny."

Reputation — what is said of us — is of little account; but character — what we are and expect to be — is the pearl of great price; it is the only solid thing in existence; it is the result of obedience to principles — "character pure, truthful, brave, unselfish, and self-sacrificing, is godlike and divine"; "it is the only object of moral reverence and spiritual ambition"; "it is the substance of things hoped for, the evidence of things not seen."

Character, crude, wrought, and in process, is the work of God in man; the world is the workshop, and time the material used in its construction. Character, the finished work, is the pure carbon of divine love, crystallized into forms of celestial beauty and use.

Eternity is the parent stock, the concrete whole, from which we, individual particles of character — the philosopher's stone — were hewn, and by the power of which we are held and bound as "living stones, fitted and joined together" in the temple of the living God.

As for Darwinism, — suppose we are nothing more nor less than regenerated monkeys, baboons and apes, if the regeneration is perfect and complete, it is no reproach; but if, on the other hand, it is hardly begun within us, and we continue (especially if we are in the pulpit) to act the "dyspeptic owl," or pious monkey, and treat our friends as though they were nothing more than religious baboons and apes, we do all that it is possible for one to do, by both precept and example, to dishonor God and disgrace the race.

We do not expect, at least for the present, that human souls will be born "big at birth," like bumble-bees, but we do expect, through the unfoldment of the law of love, and the proper development of our children's children, to escape the unpleasant flavor and disagreeable effect of sour grapes in a sense that the infant, the idiot, and the insane shall have some show for regeneration in this mundane sphere.

The authority of the Old and New Testaments depends upon the truthfulness of the statements made, the doctrines inculcated, the standpoint we occupy.

The literal church seems dead and decaying. Allegorically speaking, it has been buried three days, and, like Lazarus, is sleeping in the grave. We are approaching land : the great fish is about to disgorge, the allegorical gourd, the unproductive fig-tree, must soon wither away. We would not speak disrespectfully of the Church — it is the mother that bore us; we would give her a respectful burial in the family tomb, where "all that is of the earth — earthy," must some time go.

In behalf of suffering humanity, the Lord's poor, the " an hungered," " the thirsty," " the stranger," " the naked," " the sick," and " the imprisoned," we would invite you to the judgment-seat of Christ, the court of heaven. The court is to be holden in your own hearts and consciences; the time and place is to be the state and condition when you are sufficiently enlightened to see yourself as you are seen, and "know" as you are "known." You may plead ignorance; we answer, You have all persons, places, and things to teach you. You may plead a lack of time; we answer, You have all eternity to be taught in: take all the time you need, but come up you must, into the broad church, through the unfolding law of love implanted within you.

The church will not be full until every human soul has joined it; it will not be perfect until each individual member has perfected himself, — the divine plant, — and unfolded the fruitage of heaven.

We could extend these articles *ad finitum*, but it is useless to do so; each one must extend for himself. For working plans, detail drawings, and specifications, we would refer you to Genesis, John, and Revelation, the allegorical Father, Son, and Holy Ghost — the literal Abraham, Isaac, and Jacob of the New Dispensation.

"In a work on the *Principles of Zoölogy*, by Prof. Agassiz, there is a remarkable and interesting frontispiece, intended, as the author says, to present at one view the distribution of the principal types of animals and the order of their successive appearance in creation, as well also as the rank or grade which each maintains to the other and to all. The ingenious diagram instructs us that there have been four successive periods in the career of creation; that in the first there was the reign of fishes, in the second the reign of reptiles, in the third the reign of mammals, in the fourth the reign of man. And these various orders of animals, with their different genera and species, are ranked in the picture according to their natures, one above the other; and at the top or head of the line is placed the word MAN. He is the last creature to appear, but by no means the least. For through all the preceding stages of creation there seems to have been a preparing for him. The Creator, as we might say, was holding himself in reserve to do his best thing last, when all had been got ready for it. God, as the designer of this diagram would seem to intimate, approached His masterpiece gradually; and when air and earth and sea were in a favorable condition, and all the fauna and flora of the planet were excellently well arranged; when beings' high gradations were piled to the point where completion lacked but another touch — then the

Author of all drew again and greatly on His infinite powers, and launched from the bosom of His own being His fairest, grandest, noblest work, and capped the climax of creation with MAN, " made in the image of his maker." Prof. Agassiz fittingly indicates the culmination of the Creator's work by placing at the apex of his diagram the symbol of royalty — a crown ; which shows that man is the coronation of creation, the head and front of all the lower orders of animals."

As in zoölogy, so in theology, ethics, and religion, there are four allegorical heads, or rivers, that water the garden, so that each of the cardinal points may be well supplied. There are four sides of the city of life, or broad church, with gates upon each side, so that all may enter and learn by experience that the Lord is in it, the light thereof. There are four seasons of the year, with months in the seasons, which serves each soul as seed-time and harvest; figuratively speaking, the tree of life must bud and blossom, grow and ripen, in each individual soul before it can be garnered home. Three successive dispensations of thought, work, and worship have passed; the fourth is a repetition of all that have preceded it; it is a summing up of divine enactments — the climax — the crowning work of God, the embodiment of Himself, the millennium, in the hearts and consciences of men. In short, the Christ, the broad church, its free religion, as defined, is to the religions and churches of the world what man is to the animal kingdom — the incarnating statement of all the truths in the systems of the past — the diadem that reflects the glory of God, His love, will, and wisdom, in the image He has made.

In closing this the December number of our articles, the Reuben of the twelve tribes, the Judas of the disciples, we would encourage freedom — we would betray the Christ with a kiss, not the freedom of the tyrant to intimidate, extort, and crucify, but the freedom of the servant, to unfold, harmonize, and bless, which lifts him into the position of a friend, with capacities to perceive, appreciate, and enjoy, to occupy and inherit the kingdom of heaven with the sons of God.

Touch the sweetest chords of music,
Sing the purest songs of praise,
For in God we are eternal,
We shall live through endless days.

"IN THE LAND WHERE WE ARE GOING.

" In the land where we are going,
    When our earthly life is o'er,
Where these tired hands cease their striving,
    And these tired heart aches no more,
In that land of light and beauty,
    Where no shadow ever came
To o'ercloud the perfect glory,
    What shall be our angel name?

When the spirits who await us
    Meet us at our entering in —
With what names of love and music
    Will their welcoming begin?
Not the ones so dimm'd with earth-stains
    Linked with thoughts of grief and pain;
No; the names that mortals gave us
    Will not be our angel name.

We have heard them all too often
    Uttered by unloving lips,
Earthly care and sin and sorrow
    Dim them with their deep eclipse;
We shall change them like a garment,
    When we leave this mortal frame,
And at life's immortal baptism
    We shall have another name.

For the angels will not call us
    By the names we bear on earth;
They will speak a holier language,
    Where we have our holier birth;
Syllabled in heavenly music —
    Sweeter far than earth may claim,
Very gentle, pure and tender —
    Such will be our angel name.

It has thrilled our spirits often
   In the holiest of our dreams,
But its beauty lingers with us
   Only like the morning beams;
Weary of this jarring discord
   Which the lips of mortals frame,
When shall we, with joy and rapture,
   Answer to our angel name?"

SONG OF THE MYSTIC.

I WALK down the Valley of Silence,
   Down the dim, voiceless valley — alone!
And I hear not the fall of a footstep
   Around me — save God's and my own!
And the hush of my heart is as holy
   As hovers where Angels have flown.

   *   *   *   *

And still did I pine for the Perfect,
   And still found the False with the True;
I sought 'mid the Human of Heaven,
   But caught a mere glimpse of its blue;
And I wept when the clouds of the Mortal
   Veiled even that glimpse from my view.

   *   *   *   *

Do you ask how I live in the Valley?
   I weep, and I dream, and I pray;
But my tears are as sweet as the dew-drops
   That fall on the roses in May;
And my prayer, like a perfume from censer,
   Ascendeth to God, night and day.

   *   *   *   *

Do you ask me the place of the Valley,
   Ye hearts that are harrowed by care?
It lieth afar between mountains,
   And God and his Angels are there;
And one is the dark mount of Sorrow,
   And one the bright mountain of Prayer.

                           — *Father Ryan.*

www.ingramcontent.com/pod-product-compliance
Lightning Source LLC
Chambersburg PA
CBHW021919180426
43199CB00032B/765